## CELEBRITY BIOS

# Liv Tyler

### Danny Fingeroth

Children's Press®
A Division of Scholastic Inc.
New York / Toronto / London / Auckland / Sydney
Mexico City / New Delhi / Hong Kong
Danbury, Connecticut

Book Design: Erica Clendening
Contributing Editor: M. Pitt

Photo Credits: Cover, pp. 19, 20, 22, 30 courtesy of Everett Collection;
pp. 4, 7 © ALPHA/Globe Photos, Inc.; p. 8 © Bettmann/Corbis; p. 11
© Lynn Goldsmith/Corbis; p. 12 © Mitchell Gerber/Corbis; p. 15 © Albert
Ferreira/Globe Photos, Inc.; p. 16 © Calliope Grigorea/Corbis; pp. 25, 29
© Reuters NewMedia Inc./Corbis; p. 26 © AFP/Corbis; pp. 32, 35 © Henry
McGee/Globe Photos, Inc.; p. 36 © Cardinale Stephane/Corbis Sygma;
p. 39 © Mark L. Stephenson/Corbis

Library of Congress Cataloging-in-Publication Data

Fingeroth, Danny.
    Liv Tyler / Danny Fingeroth.
    p. cm. — (Celebrity bios)
    Discography (p. )
    Includes bibliographical references and index.
    ISBN 0-516-24335-7 (lib. bdg.) — ISBN 0-516-27859-2 (pbk.)
    1. Tyler, Liv—Juvenile literature. 2. Motion picture actors and
    actresses—United States—Biography—Juvenile literature. I. Title. II.
    Series.

PN2287.T93F56 2003
791.43'028'092—dc21

                                                        2002155014

# CONTENTS

# CHAPTER ONE

# Bebe's Girl

*"To me, music is the most fascinating art form. It can make you feel, more than any other art. Everybody has a song that makes you feel so much."*

—Liv Tyler on *planethollywood.com*

It's no surprise that Liv Tyler would be so moved by music. She's the daughter of rock-and-roll royalty. Liv's mother, Bebe Buell, was an important part of the popular-music scene since the 1970s. Bebe founded and played with several bands, including the B-Sides and the

With her charm, elegance, and beauty, Liv Tyler attracts attention almost anywhere she goes.

Gargoyles. Liv's father is Steven Tyler of the world-famous rock band Aerosmith. Her step-father Todd Rundgren is a legendary singer-songwriter.

Like other members of her family, Liv is a performer. She doesn't play guitar or sing in packed arenas, though. In fact, Liv isn't a musician at all. She's a gifted actress. Her performances have turned heads and raised eyebrows. She amazed audiences in *Stealing Beauty* and thrilled them in *Lord of the Rings*. Liv is beautiful and talented, but she keeps a level head about herself and her work.

## GROWING UP

Liv Tyler was born July 1, 1977, at Mt. Sinai Hospital in New York City. At the time, her mother, Bebe, was a model who worked for the world-famous Ford Modeling Agency. Liv's grandmother was also a model. It seems like beauty runs in the family.

# Bebe's Girl

During rough times, Liv and her mother Bebe (right) could always count on each other's support.

Liv grew up in several places around the United States, including Maine, Virginia, and New York City. She spent time with her mother, an aunt, and her grandmother. As she told Luaine Lee of the *Scripps Howard News Service,* times were not always easy: "I remember when my mom and I got our first credit card. It was a big deal." As a kid, Liv was often a hyperactive troublemaker. "I was loud and

Growing up, one of Liv's favorite TV programs was *The Brady Bunch*. However, unlike the Brady's, Liv's home life was at times a little unsettled.

obnoxious....I had the worst case of attention deficit on the face of the earth."

Liv often found herself getting into trouble. However, she found that performing onstage provided an escape. "[T]he problems that I'd had in school disappeared when I started acting. I had something to focus my time on and to discipline myself."

## THE BEST OF FRIENDS

Liv once told her friend Drew Barrymore, who was interviewing her for a magazine, that she had a fairly normal childhood. Her favorite TV shows included *The Dukes of Hazzard*, *He-Man*, and *The Brady Bunch*. For Liv, one of the most wonderful aspects of her childhood was the strong relationship she had with Bebe. It's a caring and supportive friendship. Bebe considers Liv her "proudest life achievement." She goes on to say, "I simply adore her. I'm her biggest fan, as she is mine."

Liv feels just as proud of her mom. "I love my mommy," she raves. "She's a great friend. We're a team." Growing up, Liv deeply respected and admired her mom's artistic side. She loved listening to her mother sing onstage, or looking at her on the cover of famous magazines.

Liv also loved the clothes, makeup, and jewelry that her mom kept around the house.

Before Bebe would go out, she'd tell Liv to leave her things alone. That was one order Liv couldn't obey. Once Bebe walked out the door, Liv headed straight for her mom's bedroom and bathroom. She would play with her expensive jewelry. She'd try on all of Bebe's makeup and beautiful clothing.

## DUAL DADS

Until she was nine, Liv thought her stepfather, Todd Rundgren, was her real father. She was even given Todd's last name. Todd had always taken the father role in Liv's life. Bebe and Todd ended their romance a few months after Liv's birth. Nevertheless, he and Liv continued a father-daughter relationship. Liv visited Todd frequently. "I never really lived with my fathers, Todd or Steven. It did make me feel a little different. Everyone else had a typical mom-and-dad thing going on," she said.

Although Todd Rudgren's relationship with Bebe didn't last, the rock star never failed to support and care for Liv.

One night, Liv and her mom attended one of Todd's concerts. "I was sitting there watching Todd play," recalls Liv. "I was so proud of him. You know, my dad being up there. And suddenly my mom said that she wanted to introduce me to someone." Then she followed Bebe to another part of the concert hall. Bebe pointed to a man. At first glance, Liv mistook the man for Mick Jagger's son. Bebe laughed, then

Around the time Liv learned that Steven Tyler (center) was her father, Tyler's band Aerosmith was making a comeback. This surge in popularity came thanks to the band re-recording their hit song "Walk This Way" with rap act Run D.M.C.

explained who the man was—Steven Tyler. "I connected with him immediately," Liv remembered. Long after the concert had ended, she found herself thinking about Steven constantly. She listened to every album Aerosmith had recorded. She even wrote about him in her diary.

About a year later, nine-year-old Liv went to an Aerosmith concert. There she met Steven's daughter, Mia Tyler. Liv realized that she looked a lot like Mia. She suspected that Steven might actually be her real father. Later that night, the truth was revealed to Liv. Steven was, in fact, Liv's father.

## A DARK SECRET

Why didn't Bebe or Steven tell Liv who her father was years earlier? At the time Liv was born, Steven was addicted to drugs. His addiction caused many serious problems in his life. Bebe didn't want Liv to know that her father was abusing himself. Steven agreed.

**Did you know?**

Liv has two other half-siblings: Chelsea and Taj Tyler.

He admitted in an interview that "I wasn't dad-material while I was doing all the drugs." As Liv grew up, though, Steven wanted to be a part of her life. He credits her with giving him the motivation to clean up his life and stay off drugs.

Over the years, Liv has grown closer and closer to Steven. Steven once said that the best thing Liv inherited from him "was the great art of being herself." At age twelve, Liv changed her last name to Tyler. Also, Liv learned that Steven's family is Italian. When Steven was young, he changed his last name, Tallarico, to his stage name, Tyler. Someday, Liv hopes to travel to Italy to trace her father's family roots.

These days, father and daughter are each other's biggest fans. Liv even found that her fashionable father liked to swap beauty tips with her. "We wear each other's clothes," she said. "We wear exactly the same size in jeans.

# Bebe's Girl

Once Steven beat his tragic drug problem, he turned his attention to being a great father for his two daughters.

[W]e stay up all night trading beauty tips. He knows about all the good creams and masks."

# CHAPTER TWO

# From Runway Star to a Runaway Star

*"She's just a marvelous actress. Very serious, very prepared, and very professional. I am crazy about her."*

—Director Robert Altman, speaking about Liv's acting ability

When Liv was fourteen, she met supermodel Paulina Porizkova in New York City. Paulina was a friend of the family. She was impressed with Liv's beauty and confidence. She convinced Liv to try modeling. Liv was a natural. She soon found herself on the cover of magazines such as *Seventeen*. She walked down runways,

Liv's transformation from model to motion picture starlet was as fast as it was successful.

displaying the latest styles and fashions. Suddenly, she was getting paid to play dress-up! Liv also did a number of commercial spots for television.

## LIV'S FIRST ROLES

When she was sixteen, Liv appeared in the video for the hit Aerosmith song "Crazy." It made her famous with teenagers all over the world. Steven beamed at the chance to work with his daughter.

After the video's success, Liv began auditioning for films. On her fourth audition, she got her first part. She would be working with Academy Award winning actor Richard Dreyfuss in the 1994 film *Silent Fall*. Liv enjoyed the experience so much, she decided to quit modeling to act full time. The risk soon paid off.

## STEALING THE SHOW

The movie that really got Liv noticed was 1996's *Stealing Beauty*. Superstar director Bernardo Bertolucci auditioned hundreds of

Liv's acting ability and uncommon beauty has allowed her to gain roles in blockbuster movies, such as *Armageddon*.

actresses for the lead in that movie. Out of all those talented actresses, Bertolucci chose Liv.

There was no question that Liv would be perfect for the role. After all, she was playing a young woman who was trying to figure out her father's identity. That was one mystery Liv had some experience with!

*Stealing Beauty* established Liv as a star. That year, she also worked alongside Tom Hanks in *That Thing You Do!* Hanks recalled being stunned by Liv the first time he met her.

Liv's newfound fame gave her a different life than a typical teenager. Suddenly, she was acting alongside Hollywood's hottest actors. She was traveling overseas to work in countries such as Italy and France. As she told one interviewer, "I got to do all the normal things I wanted to do, and ten thousand things more."

More movies and high praise followed. The movies included

Liv got a chance to display her tender side in this scene from *Cookie's Fortune*, with Charles S. Dutton.

the 1997 film *Inventing the Abbotts*, the 1998 blockbuster *Armageddon* (with Bruce Willis), and 1999's *Cookie's Fortune*. *Cookie's Fortune* was made by famous director Robert Altman. For Liv, the experience was wonderful. "Working with Robert Altman," Liv said, "was a…pivotal point for me. I've always been a little bit shy. It wasn't until *Cookie's Fortune* that I felt suddenly comfortable." In *Cookie's Fortune*, Liv played Emma, a rebellious woman living in a small town. She becomes involved in a tangled—and funny—murder mystery. Many people praised Tyler's performance. They also liked the chemistry between Tyler and her onscreen romantic interest, Chris O'Donnell.

Working with Altman gave Liv a feel for comedy. This came in handy when Liv worked on another comedy called *One Night at McCool's* (2001). Liv's experience with *Cookie's Fortune* helped her have a good time making *McCool's*. "It was nice to come [to work] every day for

# LIV TYLER

In *One Night at McCool's*, Liv got the chance to work alongside
Academy-Award winning actor Michael Douglas.

*McCool's*," she said. "It can be stressful some-
times, being an actor. If you have a big scene
coming up, it's like having a paper due in school.
So *McCool's* was fun. I felt very free."

## JOURNEY TO MIDDLE EARTH
Liv's talent had brought her fame. However,
with her next role, that fame would grow by

22

leaps and bounds. In 2001, Liv began to delight moviegoers everywhere, playing the role of Arwen in the blockbuster *Lord of the Rings* trilogy. The trilogy has become one of Hollywood's greatest box-office successes.

In the films, Arwen is a three-thousand-year-old elf-princess! Trying to prepare for this unique role left Liv scratching her head. For a while, she didn't know where to begin. "How am I going to play a three-thousand-year-old?" she remembered thinking. Liv soon discovered the answer to her problem. "I realized that what makes the elves so powerful is this inner calm. It's like being the most perfect person you can be. Like someone who meditates all the time. A Buddha."

What is Liv's take on Arwen's role in the trilogy? As she told the *Los Angeles Daily News*, "She's in love with the mortal man Aragorn. But her father, Elrod, is trying to discourage their romance. Arwen is willing to sacrifice her immortality to be with Aragorn."

# LIV TYLER

Director Peter Jackson also felt the role's romantic angle was an important one. "Arwen represents a very important value of Tolkien's world, which is love," Jackson said. "She really has that incredible decision to make. Should she give up her immortality for the love of a mortal man? These are very powerful story elements."

Jackson praised Liv for doing "wonderful work" with her challenging role. Viggo Mortenson, who played Aragorn, also raved about the performance that Liv gave. "She's very relaxed and surprisingly mature," says Viggo. "She was so convincing. I honestly began imagining she really was an elf-princess."

In the *Lord of the Rings* series of books, Arwen has a minor role. However, her role was expanded for the movies. For Liv, this was a great opportunity. As she told the *Lord of the Rings Fan Club Official Magazine*, she had to "kind of wing it. Go down there and explore a lot of options. That was difficult. The thing that did

The shoot for *Lord of the Rings* was stressful and long. However, Liv grew so close with the cast and crew, they started to feel like a second family.

draw me to it most was this love story. [W]hen Aragorn dies, Arwen goes to where they met. She lies down to die, too. She's heartbroken."

By adding screen time to Liv's role, the writers felt they were improving on one part of Tolkien's novels. "The writers felt that in the book, there wasn't nearly enough of a kind of female energy," Liv told one reporter. "The only

Liv shared lots of laughs with her *Lord of the Rings* costar
Elijah Wood.

real female energy there was a big black spider
that kills everybody! But I'm part of this beautiful, romantic kind of love story. My character
has to give up immortality for love. We're these
otherworldly, amazing beings. For them, time is
a totally different thing. Fifty years is like a day."

## A STAR'S TREK

Fifty years may feel like a day to an elf, but
not to a human. The shoot for the trilogy was

a long and difficult one for the cast and crew. Finishing the shoot took two hundred and seventy-four days! That's because all three movies in the trilogy were shot at the same time. Also, most of the film was shot in New Zealand. This beautiful country was thousands of miles away from most of Liv's friends and family.

At first, Liv wasn't sure she'd be up to this demanding schedule. "I had to think really carefully if I wanted to spend a year and a half on the other side of...Earth. There were days...when I thought I couldn't go on anymore. The movie was really exhausting. But I never sat down and worried about it. I just kept going. That made me strong.

"It was different from any other movie I had experienced. It was over such a long period of time. Everything was made for the movie in New Zealand. All the special effects were done there. It wasn't until I came home [to the

United States] that I realized: 'Wow, this is gonna be kind of big!'"

Did you know?

Liv is following in her musical parents' footsteps. She sang a love song for the third *Lord of the Rings* movie. The tune will appear in the film's soundtrack.

## THE SECOND ACT

The second movie of the trilogy was released in late 2002. Like the first, it received glowing reviews. It also sold a lot of tickets. Fans loved the movies so much that many went to see them more than once! *The Two Towers* received two Academy Awards—one for Best Visual Effects, and another for Sound Editing.

The *Lord of the Rings* fanbase stretches across the entire planet. Here, a group of fans from Chile prepare to watch their favorite film.

## From Runway Star to a Runaway Star

Following the trilogy, Liv moved on to other projects. One of them was *Jersey Girl*. For this film, Liv worked alongside two of Hollywood's biggest stars (and real-life couple) Ben Affleck and Jennifer Lopez. Kevin Smith directed this movie. Smith was also the director of *Clerks* and *Chasing Amy*. *Jersey Girl* promises to be as outrageous as the rest of Smith's movies.

# CHAPTER THREE

# Liv Offscreen

*"Liv has got all the talent in the world. She also has the character to go with the talent."*

**—Steven Tyler, discussing his daughter**

Liv Tyler has already proven that she has a wealth of talent. She's shown that she can perform in many different kinds of movies. From dramas and comedies to romances and adventures, Hollywood is learning that there are few roles Liv won't try. What's more, she shows no signs of stopping.

Whether she's playing an elf-princess or a woman searching for her roots, Liv brings great sparkle and life to the characters she portrays.

## UNSPOILED BY SUCCESS

Liv has enjoyed great success and fame at an early age. Even so, most people who know her describe her as down-to-earth. Even though she earns a lot of money from acting, she prefers to live a simple life. "I don't go out that much," Liv insisted in one interview. "I don't live a very posh life. I don't have...people doing everything for me."

Liv has won praise and admiration for her kindness, charm, and positive outlook on life. She's said that dishonest people annoy her. "I'm really good at seeing through them when they're trying to tell me

## Did you know?

For the movie *Armageddon*, Liv actually stayed and lived on an oil rig for a full week!

things that aren't true." Some Hollywood actors have a reputation for arrogance. Liv, on the other hand, is humble about her talents.

Liv spends much of her time in New York City. "What I like most about being in New York is that I can just be a normal person. I just run around and do all my things." She knows that many people believe that New Yorkers can be cold. She believes this opinion is untrue. Liv thinks that most New Yorkers are generous and kind. It gives Liv lots of joy to rattle off her reasons for loving the city. "I like how unpredictable it is," she's said. "[People] have to help each

Some things never change: Bebe and Liv still love to dress up in the best fashion and attend great parties.

other. There's so much diversity. There's so much in one place. People come [here] from all over the world to live [their] dreams."

## ROMANCE WITH ROYSTON

Of course, Liv doesn't spend all her days and nights on movie sets. She has a life outside of her acting career.

For a while, Liv's boyfriend was actor Joaquin Phoenix. She fell head over heels for Joaquin when they were working together in the film *Inventing the Abbotts*. Liv discussed the relationship with Luaine Lee of *Scripps Howard*. "I fell in love for the first time in my life when I met Joaquin. We have a wonderful connection." Liv's relationship with Joaquin eventually ended. However, they remain close friends.

She started dating Englishman Royston Langdon in the summer of 1998. Three years later, they became engaged. That romantic

Not long after Liv and Royston Langdon were engaged, Royston's father revealed his hope that the two might marry in Royston's hometown in northern England.

occasion happened on February 14, 2001— Valentine's Day.

Not surprisingly, Royston is a musician. Until recently, he was the lead singer of the rock band Spacehog. In April 2001, Spacehog released their third album, *Hogyssey*. Royston wrote most of the songs. "Liv in many ways has been my inspiration and muse for this record," he said. "[T]here might not have been a record without her."

Spacehog is no longer playing together as a group. Royston, however, is writing batches of new songs, with plans to release a new record in the near future.

## ROUGH PATCH

Liv and Royston went through some tough times during the *Lord of the Rings* shooting. Liv had to stay in New Zealand through the

entire shoot. This kept her thousands of miles away from her sweetheart. Spending so many months apart was a difficult challenge for the young couple.

They weren't the only couple in the cast suffering, however. In one interview, Liv said she watched a few relationships split apart "because of the distances involved." While Liv and Royston were worried that being apart would take its toll, their relationship survived the experience. "If anything," Liv told *teenhollywood.com*, "the separation made us stronger. But at the time, it was still too long and it felt wrong."

On March 25, 2003, the couple took the plunge and got married. They decided to have a small, private wedding. The ceremony took place in the Carribean. After the ceremony, Liv presented her musical husband with a great wedding gift—a vintage Les Paul guitar. The couple certainly seems ready to make this

Liv was proud of her work in *Lord of the Rings*, and stunned by its beauty. She called it "the best film I'd ever been in."

commitment. "Beside her," Royston has said, "I am a stronger man."

Liv echoes her husband's outpourings. "I'm madly in love," she has said. "It's amazing to be able to feel, three years later, more in love than I did even when we first met."

## ON THE HORIZON

Liv's got plenty of hobbies to keep her busy when she's not acting. She loves music, of course. She also loves toys, antiques, cooking, painting, and swimming.

Of course, she's still going to continue to act. There's a rumor that Liv may soon star in a film biography of a glamorous model from the 1950s. So far, the movie has hit a few snags. It has had difficulty getting off the ground. It's one of Liv's dream projects, though, so she hopes to see it through.

One thing's for sure: Liv's going to keep on

making movies. "I don't want to just make five films...and be done," she told the *Chicago Tribune*. "I want to be like Maggie Smith or Vanessa Redgrave, make lots of films... and even greater ones when my hair is gray."

Liv is giving herself a big goal to shoot for. The odds are she'll achieve it.

Like her famous father, most people believe that Liv has a long career ahead of her.

39

**1977**   • Liv is born on July 1 in New York City as Liv Rundgren.

**1986**   • Liv is told her real father is Steven Tyler.

**1989**   • Liv changes her last name from Rundgren to Tyler.

**1991**   • Liv begins modeling.

**1993**   • Liv appears in Aerosmith's "Crazy" video.

**1994**   • Liv makes her acting debut in the films *Silent Fall* and *Heavy*.

**1995**   • Liv appears in *Empire Records*.

**1996**   • Liv stars in her breakthrough film *Stealing Beauty*.
          • Liv costars with Tom Hanks in the film *That Thing You Do!*

**1997**   • Liv is chosen by *People* magazine as one of the 50 Most Beautiful People in the World.

# TIMELINE

**1998**
- Liv stars in *Armageddon*.
- Liv begins dating rock personality Royston Langdon.
- Liv appears in the film *Cookie's Fortune*.

**2001**
- Liv stars in *One Night at McCool's*.
- Liv appears in *Lord of the Rings: The Fellowship of the Ring*, playing the role of elf-princess Arwen Undómiel.
- Liv and Royston are engaged on Valentine's Day.

**2002**
- Liv continues her role as Arwen in *Lord of the Rings: The Two Towers*.
- Liv begins filming *Jersey Girl* with director Kevin Smith.

**2003**
- The last episode in the *Lord of the Rings* trilogy is released.

# FACT SHEET

| | |
|---|---|
| **Name** | (original) Liv Rundgren, (current) Liv Tyler |
| **Born** | July 1, 1977 |
| **Birthplace** | New York City |
| **Family** | Mother, Bebe Buell; father, Steven Tyler; "spiritual" father, Todd Rundgren; half-sisters, Mia and Chelsea; half-brother, Taj |
| **Nickname** | Liver |
| **Height** | 5'10" |
| **Hair** | Brown |
| **Eyes** | Blue |
| **Sign** | Cancer |

## Favorites

| | |
|---|---|
| **Hobbies** | Music, toys, antiques, shopping, painting, and swimming |
| **Musicians** | David Bowie, Patsy Cline, Hank Williams, Marvin Gaye, Edith Piaf, Dinah Washington, Etta James |
| **TV Show** | *The Late Show With David Letterman* |
| **Friends** | Jade Jagger, Claire Danes, Kate Moss, Drew Barrymore, Gwyneth Paltrow, Kate Hudson |
| **Fashions** | Ghost, Trashy, Tracy Feith, Marc Jacobs, Dolce & Gabanna, Paul Smith, Sonia Rikyel, Chanel, Dior |
| **Restaurants** | Brown Bag Food Company (East Hampton, New York), Salt & Battery (New York City) |

# NEW WORDS

**abusing** (uh-**byooz**-ing) treating a person or creature cruelly

**arrogance** (**a**-ruh-guhns) conceit

**aspects** (**as**-pekts) the features or characteristics of something

**audition** (aw-**dish**-uhn) a short performance by an actor to see whether he or she is suitable for a part in a play or film

**Buddha** (**boo**-duh) the name given to Siddhartha Gautama, the Indian teacher who founded the religion of Buddhism

**gargoyles** (**gar**-goilz) stone heads or figures carved below the roof of old buildings

**hyperactive** (hye-pur-**ak**-tiv) when a person is unusually restless and has difficulty sitting quietly

**immortality** (ih-mor-**ta**-luh-tee) the state of living or lasting forever

**misconception** (miss-kuhn-**sep**-shuhn) a view or opinion of something that is incorrect

**motivation** (moh-tih-**vay**-shuhn) encouragement to do something

**muse** (**myooz**) someone or something that provides a person with creative inspiration

**pivotal** (**piv**-uh-tuhl) a key moment or important event in someone's life

**posh** (**posh**) very stylish or expensive

**trilogy** (**tril**-uh-jee) a group of three related movies that make up a series

## FOR FURTHER READING

Boulais, Sue. *Liv Tyler*. Bear, DE: Mitchell Lane Publishers, Inc., 2000.

Sibley, Brian. *The Lord of the Rings: The Making of the Movie Trilogy*. New York: Houghton Mifflin, 2002.

Sibley, Brian. *The Lord of the Rings Official Movie Guide*. New York: Houghton Mifflin, 2001.

## WEB SITES

**The Internet Movie Database — Liv Tyler Page**
*http://us.imdb.com/Name?Tyler,+Liv*
The Internet Movie Database Web site provides information on all your favorite celebrities. Check out Liv's IMDB page to find out about her upcoming projects.

**The Liv Tyler Online Shrine**
*www.online-shrine.com/tyler/*
On this Web site, get the latest updates on Liv. Plus, click on links to pages about some of her friends—including *Lord of the Rings* costar Elijah Wood and ex-beau Joaquin Phoenix.

**The Lord of the Rings Official Site**
*www.lordoftherings.net/index_flat.html*
The features on this site can take you deep in the heart of Middle Earth.

**LOTR Official Fan Site**
*www.lotrfanclub.com/*
Think you know Hobbits? This link is packed with so much information about the trilogy, you'll be a Hobbit scholar by the time you finish surfing the site.

# INDEX

# INDEX

## ABOUT THE AUTHOR

Danny Fingeroth was the editor of Spider-Man comics at Marvel comics for many years. He helped create the Spider-Man animated series in the mid-1990s. He has written hundreds of comic books and several prose novels.

# DATE DUE

| | | | |
|---|---|---|---|
| FEB.16.2005 | SEP.05.2005 | | |
| FEB.23.2005 | SEP.28.2006 | | |
| MAR21.2005 | OCT.05.2006 | | |
| APR.12.2005 | OCT.16.2006 | | |
| APR.20.2005 | OCT.30.2006 | | |
| APR.27.2005 | NOV.14.2006 | | |
| MAY 16.2005 | NOV.30.2006 | | |
| OCT.20.2005 | JAN.03.2007 | | |
| | JAN.17.2007 | | |
| NOV.08.2005 | | | |
| DEC.06.2005 | JAN.26.2007 | | |
| JAN.03.2006 | MAR02.2007 | | |
| JAN.23.2006 | MAR12.2007 | | |
| FEB.02.2006 | SEP.26.2007 | | |
| MAR.15.2006 | SEP.28.2007 | | |
| MAR27.2006 | JAN.18.2008 | | |
| APR.18.2006 | JAN.24.2008 | | |
| APR.26.2006 | | | |
| MAY 12.2006 | | | Printed in USA |